WALK WITH ME

Discover Hoyt Arboretum
in Portland, Oregon

By David Boe

Text copyright © 2020 David Boe
All Rights Reserved

ISBN: 978-0-9977569-2-0

DEDICATION

*For my adorable, beloved best friend,
my dog, Buddy, who has been at my side
every step of the way, including every keystroke
as I researched, wrote, and recorded this book.*

CONTENTS

DEDICATION 3
PREFACE 5
1. THE VISITOR CENTER LOOP...6
2. THE OVERLOOK TRAIL...11
3. PORTLAND'S AMAZING WATER SUPPLY 13
4. THE VIEWPOINT AND MOUNT ST. HELENS 14
5. THE RESERVOIR LOOP..20
6. THE MAGNOLIA TRAIL AND THE LOVER TREE.............23
7. THE WINTER GARDEN 30
8. UP THE WILDWOOD TRAIL...32
9. THE CLEARING BECAME STUMPTOWN, THEN PORTLAND 35
10. THE DAWN REDWOOD 38
11. THE REDWOOD DECK...43
12. THE CREEK TRAIL AND BRISTLECONE PINE TRAIL......46
13. JAPANESE LARCH, THE BAMBOO FOREST, AND THE NORWEGIAN WOOD 55
14. THE LIGHTNING TREE 58
15. ACKNOWLEDGEMENTS 61
16. DISCLAIMER..62

PREFACE

This book grew out of a challenge that presented itself when I wanted to turn a hike in Portland's Hoyt Arboretum into an "Airbnb Experience."

I was intrigued when I first heard about the concept, and immediately seized on the idea of offering a guided visit through the lovely park that sits less than half a mile from my front door.

But I stopped short when I saw that in order to qualify as something that Airbnb would offer, the experience would need to be a "life-changing" event.

I've lived within a half-mile of the arboretum for more than twenty years. I've used the park's beautiful trails like an extended backyard and always appreciated my good fortune. But like many locals, I had never taken much time to look beneath the surface. When I did, I was frankly astonished by what I found.

This book is intended to walk you through the park along the trails that I have walked with hundreds of visitors over many years. It also serves as the script for the audiobook version, which I have personally recorded.

Seeing the arboretum's magic through the eyes of hundreds of first-time visitors has given me a singular perspective on this crown jewel among Portland's many parks. Let me share with you what I found along the way. Walk with me!

1. THE VISITOR CENTER LOOP

Reference Point - Welcome Panel
Directly in front of the Visitor Center
4000 SW Fairview Boulevard
Portland, OR 97221
Hoyt Arboretum Map

Greetings, and welcome to Hoyt Arboretum. I start my hikes at the large interpretive welcome panel/site map that sits directly in front of the visitor center. Colorful welcome panels like this are found at key entrance points to the park. The welcome panels are identical except for the "You Are Here" indication on the map.

Along with more than two dozen other subject-specific interpretive panels found at various points around the park, these panels provide detailed information about the specific location we're visiting. Throughout the book, you'll find them to be handy reference points to help you find your way through the park.

On this first welcome panel, you will see several different hikes highlighted. There is a half-hour loop, a one-hour loop, and a two-hour loop. What I've done with my hike is to combine many of the best things from each of those loops into a single hike that covers a little more than 3 miles and takes between 2 to 2½ hours.

Before we step into the park itself to discover some of the most interesting trees you'll ever see, look up. Planted just behind the welcome panel is a ginkgo biloba tree, also known as a maidenhair tree. Look at its distinctive fan-shaped leaves; they're very different from the leaves of any other tree, and they turn bright yellow in fall.

Just to our right is a fig tree, with the distinctive fig leaves that you may have seen covering Adam and Eve's private parts in works of art related to Bible stories. Look at the little black plaque that's attached to or near each of these trees to find more information. We'll talk more about these little plaques shortly.

Directly behind us, a little toward the street, you'll find one of the rarest trees in the arboretum, a Wollemi pine, of which there remain only about 100 known mature examples in the world today. Due to habitat loss, climate change, and the tree's slow reproductive cycle, these trees are all but certain to become extinct in the wild.

Turn back toward the interpretive panel and walk just to the left of it to find the first trail, the Visitor Center Loop, which is paved and ADA-compliant. While this won't be the case for the vast majority of the hike, the first very small section of about a quarter-mile loop is entirely wheelchair accessible. We'll use the paved Visitor Center Loop to take us to our first dirt trail, the Beech Trail. Along the Visitor Center Loop, however, there are already some interesting things to point out about the arboretum in general.

An arboretum is in fact a library of trees, a living museum. It's also a tremendously valuable resource, in that many of the trees in the arboretum were actually planted here. The origin of the seeds from which they came is known and recorded, and much of this information is publicly available online.

The very first large tree we come to, however, is not one that was planted. If you look on the black plaque that you'll find on many trees in the arboretum, you'll see some information, including the common name, Douglas fir, the Latin or Latinized name, (Pseudotsuga menziesii), its native range, and a series of numbers that indicate its location within the park. At the lower right, you will also see a large N, which stands for Native. This tells us that this tree was not planted here; rather, it grew here naturally, and it pre-dates the 1928 founding of the park.

On other trees, in place of the letter N, you'll find a set of numbers. In many cases, the last two digits will indicate the year that the tree was planted. Note that these tree ID plaques are produced by the arboretum and have evolved over many years. They don't all have the same format, and sometimes, the year of planting may not be shown. A long-term goal of the arboretum is to update and standardize all of these little plaques.

The Douglas fir is Oregon's official state tree, and a fun statistic is that in just about any forest in Oregon other than the arboretum, if you reach out and touch a tree at random, eight out of ten times it will be a Douglas fir. They are incredibly common and grow like weeds in Oregon, Washington, and British Columbia. We'll talk more about them along the way.

Reference Point
INTERPRETIVE PANEL - OAK
Along the Visitor Center Loop

The first interpretive panel we will come to along the Visitor Center Loop highlights five of the varieties of oak trees that are planted here. In addition to the small "You Are Here" map on the left side, the panel is full of colorful photos, drawings, and detailed descriptions of the trees and their distinctive flowers, fruits, foliage, and bark. Near to the sign is a bur oak that was planted in 1972, for example, and there is also a white oak and an English oak that were both planted in 1973.

It's fun and interesting to seek out the small black plaques on Hoyt Arboretum trees. We can learn what kind of tree it is, its natural habitat, and often, using the year it was planted, we can figure out how old it is. I've become so spoiled by them that I catch myself looking for them when I'm not in the park!

In the early 1900s, when the idea for an arboretum in Portland was first discussed, it was the accepted practice for arboretums to group similar trees together. This means that instead of just one or two examples of a particular tree, we'll often find several—or even, as we'll see along a couple of interesting trails, an entire forest that would seem to have been uprooted from its native land and transplanted here in Portland.

Continue along this paved trail. On a clear day in winter, when there are no leaves on the trees, and if you know exactly where to look, you can catch a glimpse of Mount St. Helens when seated at the park bench at about the halfway point of the Visitor Center Loop. Most of the year, however, this view is totally obscured by leafy trees.

Soon after the bench, we come upon a large tree from China known as a Tree of Heaven, planted in 1937. These trees are also known as the Tree of Hell, in part because they have a tendency to create substantial thickets that spring up from the roots. It's perhaps for this reason that the tree was planted close to the arboretum's office, where the team can keep an eye on it so it doesn't get out of hand.

An interesting fact about this tree is that it figures prominently in a famous piece of American literature. This is the tree from Betty Smith's A Tree Grows in Brooklyn, published in 1943, which was the best-selling book of WWII. Naturally, it also became a very popular movie with the same name. Made in 1945, it starred actors most people don't remember anymore, but they were among the most famous of their day: Dorothy McGuire, Joan Blondell, and James Dunn, who won an Oscar. It was Director Elia Kazan's first movie; he later became famous with several movies that often figure on all-time best lists of American cinema: *A Streetcar Named Desire, East of Eden,* and *On the Waterfront.*

In the book, which some scholars consider one of the Great American Novels, the Tree of Heaven is a metaphor for the American spirit. In that regard, it checks a lot of boxes: It's an immigrant—in this case, Chinese—and it has a tremendously strong will to survive and thrive, often in less-than-optimal conditions. The author specifically chose this tree because it is known for these qualities.

As we continue along the paved trail as it loops back toward the Visitor Center, we also pass underneath several Chinese cork trees, which are particularly beautiful. But as promised, we won't stay on the blacktop for long. Just before the next right turn on the paved path, we'll take a left onto a dirt path, a short connector trail that leads to the Beech Trail, named for the various beech trees planted there. It's just a few steps down the hill.

Turn left onto the Beech Trail and continue a few more steps down the hill to find one of the most unusual of the many individual trees that we'll see today. It's literally the first large tree on the right that you come to as you head down the hill, about a dozen steps from the connector trail. I mention this because if you're not careful, you could walk right past it (as I did for many years) without even noticing.

This is a weeping beech, planted in 1941. Look carefully, and you'll find a narrow little path that leads steeply down the hill into the tree. From the Beech Trail, the tree's trunk is visible only in winter when there are no leaves. The rest of the year, this tree creates its own special secret fort, and the little path disappears into what looks like a thicket of leaves.
Be careful when stepping down into that thicket of leaves, and watch out for the little black ID plaque mounted in the ground. It's easy to trip over.

This tree is quite unusual for a beech tree. On a regular beech tree, the branches extend out and up. But this tree is a mutant, a mutation of a regular beech tree that was discovered in England in the 1830s.

People enjoyed the privacy that you find when you plunge down into it to find the trunk. Soon, professional garden designers began to recommend it in various settings and made copies of it by taking cuttings from the original tree. Such cuttings create clones that grow into a new tree with the same characteristics as the parent tree.

This weeping beech has become popular all over the US, and every weeping beech in America is descended from a single tree that was brought over from England in 1847. Standing next to the trunk, notice how the cascading long limbs and dense leaves create a completely private space, like a secret fort. Hidden here, you can't even see the trail just a few feet away!

After our excursion into the weeping beech, head back up the path to the trail, turn left up the hill, and take a look at some more traditional beech trees. These are examples of European beech trees. Interestingly, the origin of the word "beech" is believed to come from the Celtic word for "book." Some of the earliest human writing was done on tablets made of beech wood.

Continue up the hill toward the Visitor Center parking lot, with the European beech trees on our left. From the parking lot, we'll keep left along the sidewalk to another paved trail that leads up the hill. This is the Overlook Trail.

2. THE OVERLOOK TRAIL

DOUGLAS FIR, BIG LEAF MAPLE, AND MADRONE

Reference Point
Blacktop, wide paved trail, a
few steps from the parking lot,
beginning of the Overlook Trail

At the base of the Overlook Trail, you'll see another welcome panel like the one we saw in front of the Visitor Center. Continue to walk up the paved section, past the tall Douglas fir, toward another large native tree, a beautiful big leaf maple tree. Both of these large trees pre-date the park, and the big leaf maple tree is probably more than 200 years old—a beautiful specimen indeed.

From directly in front of that big maple tree, we have a good perspective from which to look back down the hill at the tall Douglas fir. Do you notice anything unusual about it? Unlike most trees, it doesn't have any branches on the lower portion of the tree. Moreover, it looks like there never were any branches; there's perhaps 50 feet of bare tree trunk before you reach the lowest branches. Why do you suppose that is?

It turns out that the needles of a Douglas fir are remarkably *in*efficient at converting sunlight into energy. If they encounter too much shade, the branches simply die and fall off. This forces the tree to grow taller in search of sunlight, and as it does, it also grows in a way that makes it look as if there never were any branches.

From a commercial standpoint, this makes the tree extraordinarily valuable, because it means that there are significant sections of wood in which there is no evidence of branches, or knots. Knots, in commercial wood products, represent points of weakness. You may have seen a wood plank or a piece of plywood with loose knots in it. In some, you can actually push the knot out. But in large sections of wood from Douglas fir trees, there are no knots at all, which helps to make the wood unusually strong.

Doug firs (as they're often called, for short) are also naturally very strong and pliable. As tall trees, they have to be able to bend in the wind. And because wildfires are an important part of their native ecosystem, they're naturally fire resistant, as well.

Using modern construction techniques, including something called Cross Laminated Timber, or CLT construction, it's now possible to use wood in place of steel and concrete in construction of high-rise buildings. There is a 12-story high-rise building located in downtown Portland constructed using such techniques, and much taller buildings in the works, including a projected 70-story skyscraper in Tokyo.

Wooden structures built in this way have the benefit of being as strong as or stronger than concrete or steel. Since they're made from renewable resources, they can also be cheaper. As mentioned, Douglas fir is naturally fire resistant, and even earthquake resistant, since wood is more flexible than steel or concrete.

At this point, we're still in front of the beautiful big leaf maple. This is a native tree that has the largest leaves of any maple; they can be up to a foot or more across! These trees produce a very beautiful hardwood that is used for furniture and many other things such as musical instruments, like guitars and pianos. And they have the world's oldest helicopters; maple seeds are kids' favorites.

I've often been surprised on my hikes to pick up one of these mini-helicopters and demonstrate it to a visitor who had never seen one. You'll often find them strewn about by the wind in this part of the park.

The seed pods, called samara—meaning dried fruit—are edible and were a valuable food source for Native Americans.

Facing the big leaf maple, directly behind us, just a little bit farther up the hill, are several native madrone trees. If you go up about another dozen steps, there's one that is close enough to the trail to reach out and touch the smooth trunk, light green in color, and remarkably cool, even in summer, so much so that it's been nicknamed the "refrigerator tree."

Continue up the trail to the top of the hill. On a clear day, as you walk up the trail and glance to the left, you will have a spectacular view of Mount St. Helens. That view will be even better when we reach the viewpoint. Before we get there, though, let me tell you about the huge water reservoir that's coming up at the top of the hill.

3. PORTLAND'S AMAZING WATER SUPPLY

You always know when you're near the top of a hill in Portland because this is where you'll find the huge water reservoirs. Portland has 64 tanks constructed of either concrete or steel. The tanks hold from 60,000 to 4 million gallons of water. This tank is the largest of the three found in the arboretum; it holds 3 million gallons.

There's a fascinating story behind Portland's water supply and the ingenious engineering that uses only gravity to bring water to the city. Early in its history, city managers realized that 26 miles east of Portland is a rainforest, where it rains more than 130 inches per year.

Beginning in the 1890s, construction began on the Bull Run watershed, where today, reservoirs hold 17 billion gallons of rainwater runoff and provide some of the purest water of any municipal water system on Earth—so pure, in fact, that for more than the first 100 years of operation, it barely needed any type of water purification or treatment at all, aside from basic filtration to get the pine cones out.

It was only after the local service area grew to over 1 million people, and the Bull Run source needed to be supplemented with groundwater and river water, that more advanced water treatment facilities were built.

At the top of the hill next to the giant water tank, we'll make a hairpin right turn and keep to the right on the trail to find the viewpoint.

This is the highest point in the arboretum and one of the highest points in the City of Portland itself, at an elevation almost 900 feet above sea level. Just 3 miles away, the elevation of the Willamette River as it flows through downtown Portland is only 30 feet above sea level, more than 850 feet lower. On a clear day you'll enjoy one of the most spectacular views in town of Mount St. Helens. On really clear days you can also see Mount Rainier, peeking out from behind the left shoulder of Mount St. Helens.

4. THE VIEWPOINT AND MOUNT ST. HELENS

You'll know you've reached the viewpoint when you see the set of three interpretive panels. Appropriately, these panels are mounted atop rock pillars made from Columbia River basalt, a volcanic rock that formed millions of years ago from lava flows. Each of these panels provides interesting historical background about the arboretum, which I won't repeat here. Instead, I encourage you to read them when you visit.

The middle panel is packed with information about the four significant volcanoes within 100 miles of Portland: Mount St. Helens and Mount Hood, both within about 50 miles; Mount Adams, 76 miles away, and Mount Rainier, about 100 miles away. All of them are potentially active and could literally go off at any time, with Mount Rainier being the largest and by far the most dangerous, since so many people live on or near it.

I'll focus on Mount St. Helens, since I was in Portland when it erupted, and I can offer my own eyewitness account.

Mount St. Helens takes its English name from a British diplomat who never saw it or even set foot in the Pacific Northwest, Lord St. Helens. He was a friend of explorer George Vancouver, who made a survey of the area in the late 1700s. In some ways this is pretty unfortunate, since the native Klickitat populations had other names for it: Loowit, or Louwala-Clough, which roughly translates to "smoking mountain" or "fire mountain."

I say unfortunate because it's possible that many lives could have been spared if we'd had a better appreciation of the oral histories and native wisdom of the people who lived in this area for thousands of years before European settlers arrived in force in the 1800s and began naming things left and right, without considering the stories that natives actually tried to explain to them, and that the Louwala-Clough volcano in particular had an especially explosive history.

I remember the first time I saw Mount St. Helens. My family moved to Oregon in 1967, when I was 10. We moved into a big, terribly run-down old house that my father had bought for $20,000, in Portland's West Hills. At that time, before the trees he planted in the backyard grew tall enough to obscure the view, Mount St. Helens, Mount Hood, and Mount Adams were all visible from the back side of the house.

I remember first thinking that the most beautiful of those must be the famous Mount Hood I had heard about, the tallest mountain in Oregon. I reasoned that it had been so named because it looked like the smooth hood of a jacket, with a gently rounded top that gave it a friendly, welcoming appearance. It was so tall that it wore its white snowcap all summer long and had a playful look to it, like a child's drawing of a mountain.

I remember being disappointed to learn that Oregon's Mount Hood was instead the craggy, pointy peak to the south, and that Mount St. Helens wasn't even in Oregon, but 50 miles north in the state of Washington.
I'm far from the only person to have noticed the mountain's symmetry and balance. For many years, Mount St. Helens was known as the "American Mount Fuji" and was widely admired for the stunning, perpetually bright glow of light reflected from the glaciers that covered it all year round.

I was a young adult, thirteen years later, when Mount St. Helens blew its top, and the date of May 18, 1980 is one that I'll never forget.

Portlanders of the time weren't entirely surprised by the eruption; we knew that something was going on.

Mount St. Helens is visible from many places around town, and it had started huffing and puffing back in March of that year, sending up clouds of steam and ash, and leaving an ugly black spot halfway up its side, like some kind of giant pimple. Its usual perfect symmetry was ruined, and I was eager for the volcanic episode to end, so that the snow and ice could cover the ugly spot and we could have our perfect mountain back again.

Alas, it was not to be, and at 8:32 a.m. on Sunday, May 18, the unimaginable happened.

It's no exaggeration to say that it was unimaginable. Of the 57 people who were killed in the initial blast, one was Dave Johnston, a volcanologist who was near the danger zone. He was one of only a small handful of people in the world who had any idea how dangerous the mountain really was. The fury unleashed that day was unlike anything anyone had ever seen, and no one was prepared for what happened.

It started with a rumble from below. An earthquake measuring 5.2 on the Richter scale caused the mountaintop to shear off, sending thousands of tons of snow, ice, and at least a century's worth of accumulated glaciers barreling down the mountainside at speeds of up to 150 miles per hour.

At this point, barely ten seconds had elapsed, but we were already in uncharted territory: the shearing-off of Mount St. Helens' perfectly symmetrical mountaintop was the largest avalanche that anyone had ever seen, the largest debris avalanche in recorded history. In the space of just a few seconds, Mount St. Helens went from the fifth-highest peak in the state of Washington to the 52nd, losing 1,313 feet in elevation.

Johnston, the USGS scientist assigned to watch the mountain that day, was apparently initially thrilled to witness this once in a lifetime event from his monitoring station six miles from the summit. The volcanologist had switched shifts that day so his colleague could have that Sunday off. He had time to make a radio call to the US Geological Survey office in Vancouver, Washington.
"Vancouver, Vancouver! This is it!" were his last words.

Johnston was one of the leading volcano experts in the world, and he knew the dangers. In fact, after some tremors a day earlier, he told a fellow geologist who was supposed to be monitoring the mountain with him that day to go home, saying that he would watch the mountain alone.

When the mountaintop sheared off, it exposed cool Pacific air to the huge pool of lava that had been accumulating for many months. It immediately became explosive, but before it erupted straight up, as many had expected, the initial blast went sideways, shooting out in a huge lateral explosive burp of superheated gas that hugged the ground, racing north, over the avalanche. Although he was six miles from the source, Johnston would have been incinerated by an enormous burst of 1,000° volcanic gas, ash, and pumice, moving faster than the speed of sound, more than 670 miles per hour.

His remains were never found, but highway workers eventually discovered the rusting hulk of his USGS trailer more than a dozen years later, in 1993.

Such explosions of gas, ash, and pumice are called pyroclastic flows. As the ice, rock, and snow avalanche caused by the earthquake tumbled down the steep mountain slope, the pyroclastic flow flashed over and enveloped it, instantly melting the snow and ice, and turning the huge quarter-mile of mountaintop into an enormous mudflow that barreled down the mountain at speeds of up to 150 mph. The gas itself was so hot, and the volume of it was so immense, that it continued to fan out along the ground, flashing much of nearby Spirit Lake and the Toutle River into steam.

The blast zone extended for more than 19 miles. Within the first 8 miles, virtually everything in its path was essentially vaporized. The energy released in the initial blast was estimated by the USGS at 7 megatons. That's 300 times the amount of energy released by the atom bomb that leveled Hiroshima. Over the course of the day, the total energy released was estimated at 24 megatons. That's 8 times the energy of all the weapons discharged during WWII, including the atomic weapons used in Japan.

After the first 8 miles, the shockwave knocked down an entire forest of old-growth trees, snapping them down like matchsticks, all neatly flattened in the same direction, pointing north. The devastation covers some 230 square miles. That's an area larger than the island of Guam and almost identical to the land mass of the city of Chicago.

All this happened in the first few seconds, before the huge avalanche of mud, called a lahar, lubricated by the thousands of tons of melted ice and snow, screamed down the mountainside, burying everything in its path. In some places the mud was 600 feet deep; the average depth of the mudslide was 150 feet.

Simultaneously, a large portion of the mountaintop fell into Spirit Lake, creating a megatsunami that reached as high as 850 feet. Imagine a tidal wave on the side of a mountain, more than 80 stories high! That's more than 1½ times the height of the tallest building in downtown Portland.

Yet on the day it went off, people didn't know any of these details. Most of the preceding facts and figures are things that I dug up on Wikipedia and the National Geologic Survey websites in my research. Frankly, I was astonished to rediscover the scale of these events.

It was all over TV and radio that day, and since it was a beautiful, crystal-clear spring morning, the mountain was clearly visible from many viewpoints around town.

After the initial explosion at 8:32 in the morning, the huge ash cloud could be seen from all over Portland. It extended some 15 miles into the atmosphere.

The best local view was from a viewpoint at the Pittock Mansion, just over a mile from here, which is where I joined a number of people who gathered to witness history. The eruption continued all day long, with the huge ash cloud boiling out of the new, mile-wide crater that was now the gaping mouth of my favorite mountain. It continued to spout an enormous column of ash for more than 9 hours.

Luckily for Portland, the winds from the Pacific were gentle that day, headed due east. And since Mount St. Helens is 50 miles north, the ash cloud missed us completely. Cities and towns farther east were not so lucky, however, and by noon, the dense cloud was feeding into the jet stream and spreading out to be many miles wide. It turned day into night in Spokane, Washington, more than 300 miles to the east, and was seen in Denver, Colorado by 10 p.m.

A fascinating fact that anyone living in Portland at the time can also confirm is that although the explosion of energy equal to some 300 Hiroshima bombs was reportedly heard as far away as Vancouver BC and even San Francisco, here in Portland, we didn't hear a thing.

Apparently, there was a "quiet zone" within at least a 50-mile radius of the volcano. There are many reports of people who witnessed the avalanche and the eruption from a safe distance who never heard anything. In one case of miraculous survival, a photographer and his group emerged unscathed because they had set up camp in a low area behind a ridge, which protected them from the blast of superheated gases. They watched the eruption, but said that it was like watching a silent movie.

Scientists have confirmed that such sonic anomalies indeed exist, and that the quiet zone extended for dozens of miles around the volcano. The silence is associated with several factors, including the humidity, air temperature at various elevations, and local topography. One theory I read stated that the sound waves went up and bounced off the stratosphere before coming back down to earth, missing Portland. However it happened, in my own experience, it missed Portland completely.

All told, the eruption was the deadliest and most economically destructive volcanic event in the history of the United States. At least fifty-seven people were killed, along with untold thousands of animals in the surrounding forest. It destroyed 250 homes, 185 miles of highway, and 47 bridges. Despite the destruction and loss of life, we can take some comfort in the knowledge that it could have been much worse. Thankfully, the eruption came on a Sunday, or the surrounding forests might have been filled with hundreds of loggers and other forest workers. Dave Johnston gave his life that day, but he had strongly argued that the volcano be kept off limits and had successfully fought powerful commercial interests to create and enlarge the danger zone, which he was working to extend. His efforts saved many lives.

5. THE RESERVOIR LOOP

After the drama of the Mount St. Helens story, it's a good time to move toward something lighter. From the viewpoint, continue along the Wildwood Trail toward the second large reservoir you see. We will pass the Holly Trail on our right and continue on a loop around the reservoir. Along the way, we'll see some of the dozens of holly plants here in the arboretum. They are particularly showy in winter when the red, white, or yellow berries become prominent.

A fun fact about berries: Although berries come in many different colors, the three basic ones are red, white, and blue. White berries are always poisonous. Red berries are sometimes poisonous; some are, and some are not. Best to stay away. Blue-colored berries are usually edible, or at least not poisonous.

(The exception that proves the rule about blue-colored berries is an extremely poisonous plant called belladonna, or poisonous nightshade, whose berries have occasionally been fatally mistaken for blueberries. Luckily, these plants are not native to North America.)

Continue along the loop until you reach the point where it starts to curve back around to the left. A couple of dozen steps through the grass, and definitely off the trail, you'll see a small stand of birch trees. This is actually an art installation called "House for Summer." The panel at its entrance describes it as a "living tree sculpture that changes with the seasons." It was created in 1987 by an artist named Helen Lessick.

One of my first guided tours through the arboretum was a large group of about a dozen people. I didn't know what to think when the request showed up on my reservation page. Usually, my tours are for groups of just two or three guests. I had never had more than five people at once, but the group organizer had written to ask if he could bring more than the maximum of ten!

I came to understand along the way, however, that on this day, the hike was a corporate team-building exercise, and that the group was in fact a team of programmers from Airbnb's IT department. After the corporate headquarters in San Francisco, Portland's Airbnb office is the company's largest, employing more than 300 people in a trendy office in old Chinatown.

On that July afternoon I shared with this very smart group of people some of the general facts that I had gathered in creating my experience, to justify the investment of time and energy to spend a couple of hours in nature, including numerous scientific studies that consistently show the many health benefits we enjoy. Fresh air, combined with the activity of walking, helps to rid the body of toxins. After just a few minutes of walking in a wooded environment, blood pressure begins to drop, tension and stress are reduced, and you're able to think more clearly.

Since most of us live in cities, it's all too easy to forget that we evolved in nature, and that it is in nature where our bodies, minds, and senses are most keenly activated. The human animal is exquisitely adapted to live in a forest environment, a reality that is plainly contrary to the life and the living memory of most who walk with me. Yet it's an undeniable common bond that we all share with every other person on earth.

On an evolutionary timescale, it was barely the blink of an eye ago that our great-great grandparents—people whose names most of us don't even know—were living and thriving in conditions that we would consider intolerable.

Anyway, on the hike with Airbnb's IT team, I gathered them into the House for Summer and joked that of all the homes in the Portland area, the only one that you couldn't potentially find on Airbnb was THIS one. They laughed, and a few of them said, in effect, "Not so fast...we could find a way...."

While we're in the House for Summer, before we head back to the reservoir loop, look behind the "house" for a large, symmetrical tree that overlooks Fairview Boulevard, just beyond it. Although not as tall as the many Douglas fir trees in the part of the park, this large tree is an especially beautiful example of one of the arboretum's signature trees, a dawn redwood.

Planted in 1950, it was in the very first batch of dawn redwood trees planted in North America. We'll be talking a lot about the dawn redwood in Chapter 10, but the placement of this particular tree allows you to walk right up to it and touch its soft needles. It's one of my favorite trees in the park, for reasons that I'll explain in detail when we visit the larger stand of redwoods.

Return to the path that we were on and continue on the loop back toward the viewpoint. Now the reservoir will be on your left, and we'll pass through a grove of a few dozen beautiful, tall Douglas firs, most of which predate the existence of the park. Virtually all of them are over 100 years old, and some of them may approach 300 years in age.

If you know where to look (and I'll tell you in a later chapter), you can find the oldest tree in the arboretum. Its age cannot be known with certainty, but it could more than 500 years old. Douglas firs can live to well over 1,000 years.

As we walk along this high point of the park, look around on the ground for some pine cones. It's actually a misnomer to call them pine cones, however, since what you'll find will be Douglas fir cones, and there's a cute story about them that forest rangers like to tell to children:

In ancient times, before humans had ever found what we now call the Pacific Northwest, there were only trees and animals. In those days, animals and trees could talk to one another. The story is about a family of mice. One day, the mouse-children wanted to run out and play in the forest. The mother mouse said, "Okay, but be sure to come back before the sun goes down, or the owl will eat you!" The little mice ran off happily and played the whole day. But soon they realized that the sun was going down and they couldn't find their way home in the dark.

Frightened, they began to cry. As the sun sank lower, the mighty Douglas fir took pity on them and said, "Don't be afraid, little ones! You can climb up my trunk and hide in the bark."

So that's what they did. And they survived the night and found their way home the next morning. Now, to commemorate their survival, when you pick up a Douglas fir cone, if you look carefully, you'll see what looks like the two hind legs and the tail of a tiny mouse, several dozen of them, hiding on every cone. This is a feature that is found only on Douglas fir cones, and it's one of the distinguishing characteristics of the tree, in addition to being a cute little forest fairy tale.

After finishing the loop around the reservoir, continue walking along the Wildwood Trail, passing the Mount St. Helens viewpoint and returning toward the first reservoir. For a few dozen paces, the Wildwood Trail merges with the Overlook Trail. However, the Wildwood Trail quickly veers off to the right, around the reservoir, and continues for more than a mile down the hill on a big loop through the woods overlooking the Japanese Garden. Our next trail, however, is the Magnolia Trail, which is clearly marked along the way.

6. THE MAGNOLIA TRAIL AND THE LOVER TREE

Reference Point
Continue straight ahead after the Wildwood Trail veers off around the reservoir. Follow the trail indicator sign that says Magnolia Trail.

Keep to the left on the trail as it widens and becomes a service road. You will immediately come upon a gated entrance to the service road. The gates are always locked, except when in use by arboretum staff. The footpath, however, passes directly alongside the gates, allowing easy, unobstructed access. At this point we will cross Upper Cascade Drive.

While crossing the road, take a look at the houses to our right. There are nine homes on the cul-de-sac, and all of them have the arboretum as their backyard. The average value found online at the time this was published was well over $1.1 million per home.

But don't stay here too long, since we didn't come to the park to discuss housing prices. Instead, head straight across the street to the Magnolia Trail. This part of the park is especially beautiful in late April and early May, when many of the arboretum's more than 120 magnolias explode with colorful blossoms.

The first trees you'll see are large California bay trees, many of which were planted in the 1960s. In southern Oregon, these trees are known as Oregon myrtle, and they are prized for their magnificent hardwood. This part of the park is a good place to notice some of the ground cover. You'll see many native ferns planted here, along with other plants such as the native blackberry with its gentle, non-threatening thorns that can be easily handled, not to be confused with the bloodthirsty Himalayan blackberry which you may also find near the top of the Magnolia Trail.

These plants were unfortunately introduced by a botanist in the late 1800s, who thought that Oregon's native blackberries were not "vigorous" enough. He was of course correct, but in those days, he had no idea that the non-native blackberries would be so terribly invasive that they can take over entire wilderness areas. Each year, arboretum volunteers haul out tons of these blackberry vines.

A delicate native plant often found along this path is the maidenhair fern, with its distinctive black stem and gentle leaves. The black stems were collected by native people and incorporated as an accent color in the baskets they wove.

There's an interesting fact about the sword ferns found here and throughout the park: Take a close look at each individual leaf. As a child, I had believed that the sword fern was so named because of the appearance of an entire fern branch. However, it's the individual leaf that gives the fern its name. If you look closely at the large end of each leaf, there's a hilt—a bump that looks like the protective handle that you would find on a full-sized sword. The sword of the fern is not the branch itself, but dozens of sword-leaves on each branch! And on the back of each individual leaf, you will find spores that spread out like dust for reproduction.

Reference Point
Magnolia Trail Interpretive Panel

Walk down the Magnolia Trail until you reach the large interpretive panel next to the tall Douglas fir tree. This panel describes many of the trees around us. The arboretum's collection of magnolia includes more than 120 specimens. Interestingly, magnolia trees evolved before bees and butterflies. They relied on beetles for reproduction, and if you get a chance to examine a magnolia flower, you'll see that the flower petals are a lot tougher and more resilient than the more fragile petals found on, say, a rose, for example. In fact, on closer inspection you'll see that the magnolia's petals look more like adapted leaves, which is what they are. In my own imagination, I see it as a way to experience experimental evolution close up. When bees and butterflies finally came along, I get a sense of an evolutionary motivation for the gentler and more spectacular types of flowers that evolved to attract them.

Interestingly, there are no magnolias that are native to Oregon. All of the arboretum's magnolia trees are native to someplace else, mostly to eastern regions of Asia and the Americas. Their beauty has made them popular all over the world.

In this part of the park you will see a number of rather odd-looking oblong square wooden structures standing about 3 feet tall. They are part of an irrigation system, which provides water during the dry summer months. Although it rains a tremendous amount here in Oregon, in June, July, and August, there's not enough rain over the summer to sustain the magnolias in our collection.

Directly behind us at the sign, a little up the hill, behind the large laurel tree, you'll find a big leaf cucumber tree a little to the right of the laurel tree. Its huge leaves can be well over a foot long; they're the largest leaves of any magnolia.

The Lover Tree

Before we leave the informational panel, however, look down the hill, straight ahead from the panel. About 100 feet in front of us, look closely at the large Douglas fir. At its base, it looks like one single tree. But about 20 feet up, you'll see that it splits into two large trunks, each one possibly over 100 years old.

I call it the lover tree because of the way the two individual trunks have become fused together, locked in an eternal embrace.

It's not at all uncommon in nature for two saplings that sprouted within a foot or two of each other to become fused together as they grow larger. They can't move, after all, so what else could they do? On a hike in nearby Forest Park, some 20 miles away, I counted two to three such double-trunked trees per mile. What's unusual and unique about this one is that the two huge trunks are intertwined like vines. But Douglas fir trees don't do this naturally. They don't behave like vines.

After years of research, including internet searches of thousands of trees all over the world, I have concluded that this particular double Douglas fir is the only one of its kind. If it isn't, it can at least be stated with certainty that it is extraordinarily rare.

This couldn't have happened by itself, and it's clear that someone or some group of people must have done this many years ago, before the nearby homes were built, and when this part of the park was more remote, less developed, and the trees themselves were smaller and somewhat more pliable.

Evidently, in the early part of the 1900s, someone, or, more likely, two or more people with a significant amount of time, strength, and resources decided to train these trees by twisting the smaller trunk around the larger one. But who, how, and why? Although I've made numerous inquiries, I have found no answers as to why or how this was done. Yet there are trails built around and directly under this unique tree, making it appear as if it was done with the knowledge of someone within the arboretum. For now, its origin remains a mystery.

There are at least two other much more typical instances of double-trunk trees elsewhere in the park. A large, very impressive specimen can be easily viewed from the Bristlecone Pine Trail, and it has a fascinating story of its own, which I'll relate when we get there.

Perhaps the most impressive view of what I call the lover tree is right at its base. Although it's allowable to go off the trail and take a closer look at almost any tree, there's a well-worn trail that passes directly underneath it, allowing a very interesting perspective. That path is about 80 more paces down the hill along the Magnolia Trail, (to our right as we face the interpretive panel). We'll find the connector trail on the left, with a trail indicator sign showing that the Beech Trail is 230 feet, and the Visitor Center .25 mile away. Before either of these, however, it rejoins the Magnolia Trail, shortly after passing directly beneath the lover tree. From there you'll be able to look directly up and see how the giant trunks intertwine.

Reference Point
From the base of the lover tree,
continue along the connector trail
in the same direction to reach
the Magnolia Trail.

Continue along the trail and pass beneath a few more magnolia trees to rejoin the main Magnolia Trail. Turn right onto the trail under the large beech trees as it winds gently toward the road, the same Upper Cascade Drive that we crossed earlier. Looking straight up the trail and across the road, we can see the weeping beech tree that we visited at the beginning of the hike.

Before reaching the road, however, you'll see a trail indicator post that points to the Beech Trail, as it goes down the hill. The Wildwood Trail is shown at 0.18 mile, and the Winter Garden is also highlighted. Turn right onto the Beech Trail and head down the hill toward the Winter Garden.

This wide, shady trail is one of my favorite parts of the park. It's hard to say exactly why, since there is nothing exceptional about this particular place. The gentle downhill slope makes it an easy place to walk, and it even feels to me as if gravity is not as strong along here, but maybe that's just an effect of the fresh air and the feeling of being so enveloped and nurtured by so many beautiful trees.

The trail curves to the right and flattens before an expansive meadow on a gentle slope that continues down the hill. Along the trail are two Japanese pendulum trees. The first one is native to Japan; the other is a garden-origin tree, but also a variant of the same Japanese pendulum tree. Both are perfectly suited to their place on the trail; one lends its gentle shade to a bench that looks over the lovely miniature valley created by the hillsides rising around it.

In summer, some giant stalks of Chilean rhubarb are often visible from that bench, just across the trail in a small gulley before the meadow that stretches out below. On sunny summer days, the expansive lawn here is quiet and inviting space, nestled into a section of the arboretum that is somewhat off the beaten track, a protected, hidden place where the light filters through the trees and the angles of the hillside combine to create a warm, welcome feeling.

The lovely meadow area here, like the Wedding Meadow we'll pass in the second half of the hike, is a design element of the arboretum that was suggested by the Olmsted Brothers, a landscape architectural firm based in Brookline, Massachusetts. Fredrick Law Olmsted is widely considered to be the father of American landscape architecture. You may have heard his name in association with New York's Central Park, which figures prominently among dozens of high-profile places that he and his sons designed or consulted on. Others include the park systems of the cities of Cleveland and Seattle, the campuses of Stanford and UC Berkeley, and park systems in Yosemite and Niagara Falls.

Olmsted's two sons, John and Frederick Jr., took over the firm from their father in 1898, and in 1905 the City of Portland commissioned a study from them for advice on how to design a great city. There are several beautiful old and well-established parks in town that can trace their origins back to the recommendations of the Olmsted Plan, including Laurelhurst Park in NE Portland; Peninsula Park, with its lovely sunken rose garden in North Portland; and the granddaddy of them all, at more than 5,000 acres, North America's largest civic park, Forest Park, which is directly connected to the arboretum via the Wildwood Trail.

Portland's very far-sighted city managers have largely followed the Olmsted Plan over the decades, and it's a significant reason why Portland has so many beautiful parks today, and why it's such an eminently livable city.

As we continue down the Beech Trail toward the Winter Garden, look back up to see the lover tree from yet another vantage point. On the long, straight section down, with the hillside to our right and the meadow to our left, we'll see a number of smaller leafy trees; many of them are native vine maples.

If you look among these smaller, smooth-trunked trees you'll notice that while many have brown-colored bark, there are also several that instead have green bark. Why do you suppose a tree would have green bark?

Before you answer, consider this: What else on a tree is green, and what do they do?

The answer is leaves, which get their green color from the chlorophyll they use for photosynthesis, which is how trees convert sunlight into energy. The reason that the bark of some smooth-barked trees is green is because it also contains chlorophyll. During the winter months when the leaves are down, these trees can still convert sunlight into energy!

7. THE WINTER GARDEN

The Winter Garden entrance is at the bottom of the Beech Trail, immediately across another neighborhood street that passes in front of the garden. It's a small section of the park that was created to highlight a few plants with unique characteristics that are best appreciated over the winter when many other plants are dormant.

At the entrance to the Winter Garden, notice the lovely white bark of the Himalayan birch trees. If you look around on the ground near these trees, you'll find what look like shavings of bark that have peeled off the tree. Pick up a piece and turn it over in your hand. It has the look and feel of a small piece of paper. In fact, it is some of the first paper used by human beings. On one of my hikes some time ago, I met a couple of visitors from India who had visited a museum in which they had seen a book written on the paper made from Himalayan birch bark; it was said to be several thousand years old.

There are a number of interesting plants in the Winter Garden, but for now, I'll focus on only a couple of them. One of the most interesting trees is found a few steps down from the Himalayan birch. The corkscrew filbert can be found just off the trail, behind the first small tree that you see on the left of the trail, a Japanese Hinoki cypress, identified by its black plaque as a Gracilus Aurea. It stands in front of the corkscrew filbert.

In summer, it may look as if the corkscrew filbert is not doing well. The leaves often look like they are wilting. This, however, is completely normal. What is much more readily apparent in winter, when the leaves are down, is that the branches of this small ornamental tree twist and turn in a very unusual fashion. During spring, summer, and fall, you must step in and push the leaves aside to be able to view the branches.

Returning to the trail, walk toward the bench a few steps farther. In late winter and early spring, the daphne plants on either side of it will offer up their incredibly sweet perfume, among the sweetest-smelling plants you'll find anywhere.

The grandest tree of the Winter Garden is the large Western red cedar, a few paces farther. Here you have the opportunity to reach out and touch the trunk of this gentle giant. Thanks to the unique molecular structure of the Western red cedar, it's almost impossible to get a sliver from one of these trees. The bark has a soft quality to it, and Native Americans used bark from these trees for a variety of things, including diapers for their newborns!

Continue through the Winter Garden and admire the various flowers and ground covers that pop up at different times of the year. At the bottom of the hill, we will turn left to rejoin the Wildwood Trail on its return from a mile-long loop down the hill. (A right turn here would take you on a lengthy loop that includes an overlook into the Japanese Garden and circles back up the hill to the giant water tank that we left earlier.) Our shorter route continues up to the left, where you will find a welcome panel a few steps away. Immediately after this point, we will cross Cascade Drive, as well as, just a few steps later, Upper Cascade Drive, as we continue along the Wildwood Trail.

8. UP THE WILDWOOD TRAIL

This will be our longest section of the Wildwood, as we rise through a steep section of the park and head back up the hill toward Fairview Boulevard. On this section of the trail, which passes a nearby residential area, you may see significant areas that are almost monoscapes of English ivy. This is ivy that has "escaped" from nearby homes and has largely taken over this part of the park. You can even see areas where the ivy is climbing trees and could eventually kill them if not properly controlled.

Since English ivy is an invasive species and has nothing to hold it back, it is very difficult to control. Every year, the arboretum's volunteer teams come in and haul out tons of various invasive species. They have worked hard to plant native ferns and other understory plants in this area, but it is an ongoing struggle against the English ivy.

Another invasive species that is often seen in this area is the Himalayan blackberry. Its thick and extremely thorny vines produce an excellent fruit, but they are also extremely hard to remove—not least because since the berries are prolific and tasty, birds feast on them and spread their seeds far and wide.

As we continue up the Wildwood Trail, look for a fist-sized blue diamond painted on a large Douglas fir tree. If you look up above it, you'll see a mileage indicator of 2¼ miles. This means that from the trailhead for the Wildwood Trail, which began back at the Vietnam Memorial adjacent to the Oregon Zoo parking lot, it is 2¼ miles from that spot. The Wildwood Trail, the longest urban hiking trail in North America, continues for another 28 ¼ miles from here.

Shortly after the 2¼-mile marker, but before we reach the top of the hill where the Wildwood Trail crosses Fairview Boulevard, we'll pause at two very interesting and unique trees: the large tanoak or tanbark oak, and a small, unusual tree called a Camperdown elm.

The tanoak is first tree we'll see. The trail comes alongside the large tree, which will be on our right. The Oak Trail continues straight ahead, but we will stay on the Wildwood Trail as it splits off to the right and continues up the hill toward the road above. This will allow us to admire the tanoak from almost every angle.

The other trees around it are also tanoaks, but they don't have the same mighty and inviting appearance. The tanoak owes its name to the high concentration of tannins found in the bark. Tannins are used in the preservation of animal skins, such as tanning leather. Before synthetic chemicals were developed that did a better job, the bark from these trees was harvested and the chemicals extracted for these types of products. The species is currently threatened by a fungus in its natural range along the southern Oregon coast.

A few more steps up the hill we'll see another informational panel, this one describing the various elm trees along the trail. One of the most unusual of these is directly behind the panel; it's called a Camperdown elm.

It's an admittedly strange name, but it makes sense once you hear the story, which is quite similar to the story of the weeping beech at the beginning of our hike. This tree is also a clone. The original tree was found in the mid-1800s on the grounds of Camperdown Estate in Scotland. Like the weeping beech that came from England, this mutant elm also had the charming feature of sending its branches cascading down in a weeping fashion. In summer, when the leaves are full and green, it's possible for several people to stand inside the small hidden area under the leaves while people walk by on the trail without even noticing.

The Earl of Camperdown's lead forester liked this tree so much that he had it moved from where it had been found in the woods to a spot that was much closer to the great manor house. If you look it up on Wikipedia, you can see a photo of the original tree from which this one was cloned.

From here, we'll continue up the hill until we reach the road and a crosswalk, which will take us across Fairview Boulevard.

9. THE CLEARING BECAME STUMPTOWN, THEN PORTLAND

When we cross Fairview Boulevard, we'll enter the conifer side of the park. The south side of Fairview (the part we're now leaving) is generally known as the deciduous side of the park. "Deciduous" refers to trees that lose their leaves in the fall and become dormant in the winter. The north side of Fairview is known for conifers, or cone-bearing trees that are usually evergreen and keep their leaves throughout the year.

That doesn't mean, however, that there are no deciduous trees north of Fairview or no conifers to the south. There are plenty of both, as we've already seen. But it is a handy way to think about the general layout of the arboretum.

This brings up some interesting facts about conifers and leaves. I learned only as an adult, researching this hike, that the needles of a conifer, such as a pine tree, or of Douglas fir tree, or the scaly, tiny shingle-like foliage of cedar trees—all of these can be correctly described as leaves. I was also surprised to learn that some of these conifers also lose their leaves (or needles) in the fall, just like the large, broad leaves of an oak or a maple tree. Such trees are called deciduous conifers, and we have a few examples of them in the arboretum, as we'll soon see.

As we walk down the path from Fairview Boulevard, we'll pass by the Wedding Meadow on our left before heading through a more heavily wooded section of the Wildwood Trail on our way to the Redwood Deck. The arboretum will sometimes host weddings or other events in the park, and I've witnessed a few such events on my many hikes.

In this section of the park, I invite guests to look at this wooded area as we walk through it and consider that (except for the invasive ivy) this part of the arboretum looks a lot like most of Portland did to the original European and American pioneers who crossed along the Oregon Trail with their covered wagons.

(Allow me to insert parenthetically that it's important to appreciate that this area was not uninhabited when white settlers arrived. Native Chinook tribes had thrived here for thousands of years, guided by a philosophy of reverence and gratitude for the land and its resources, and as a result, they left few traces. But their story is beyond the scope of this book.)

It's thought that natives may have removed the trees in a place by the Willamette River near present-day downtown, which the early pioneers called simply "The Clearing." That is the earliest reference to the place that would later be called Portland.

Here, as in many of the deep-woods sections of the Wildwood Trail, you can easily imagine how things looked when pioneer settlers arrived. Many of these people were farmers, and the first thing they did when they arrived was to start cutting down the trees on their land.

From the comfort of this gentle trail, as you look out into the dense tangle of large trees that block out the sun, consider how hard it would be, in, say, 1840, for a family with a couple of children, to clear enough land to start a vegetable garden. And what would be left over?

Stumps. By the thousand. Before the name of Portland was even considered, people called this place Stumptown. Remember, this was before mechanized equipment. The modern Caterpillar tractor (for example) wasn't built until the 1920s. Virtually all the work of clearing the land was done by hand. And stumps are the hardest things to remove. For that reason, they were usually left in place, often for years, to let nature soften them up over time. As the city grew, stumps were so dense that people used to hop from one to the next to avoid walking on the muddy, unpaved roads. From that perspective, it's easy to see why the Stumptown name caught on, and it's still used today as a stand-in for Portland: Stumptown Coffee, Stumptown Stages, Stumptown Stump Grinding.

So how did Stumptown come to be called Portland? That's also an interesting story. In 1845, there were two men who each owned 320 acres of the original 640-acre land claim of what is now downtown Portland. (640 acres is one square mile of land.) They each saw the potential for a town on their two properties, and they decided to work together to map it out. But they couldn't agree on what to call the new town. Their names were Asa Lovejoy and Francis Pettygrove.

These names are still familiar to Portlanders today, since two major streets (among other things around town) are named after them in Northwest Portland's Alphabet District, where the streets run in alphabetical order.

Asa Lovejoy was born near Boston, Massachusetts, and Francis Pettygrove, many miles north, in Maine. Both had arrived in the Oregon Territory in the early 1840s, and Lovejoy wanted to name his new hometown Boston, while Pettygrove wanted to call it Portland. Since they held equal naming rights, they agreed to settle it with a coin toss, best two out of three.

You know the rest: Pettygrove won the toss, and Portland, Oregon was named after Portland, Maine. In his will, Pettygrove bequeathed the coin they had used—a large copper penny, about the size of a 50-cent piece today—to the Oregon Historical Society. You can see what's now known as "The Portland Penny" on display in the downtown museum of the Historical Society, in a dedicated showcase in the lobby; you don't even have to buy a ticket to see it.

In retrospect, it's only fair that Pettygrove won the coin toss. He had paid $50 for his 320 acres. Lovejoy, on the other hand, had gotten his half of an original 640-acre claim for a mere 25 cents.

There's a charming extra chapter to the Lovejoy-Pettygrove partnership that stretches all the way into the 20th century. More than 110 years after they joined forces to create the city, as part of a downtown urban renewal project in the 1960s, two small tracts of land from the original 640 acres were set aside as parks; one to be named for Lovejoy, the other for Pettygrove. Today, the grass mounds, trees, paths, and stonework of Pettygrove Park sit about 300 yards away from the more prominent Lovejoy Fountain Park, which includes several water features and is popular in the summer.

When it came to deciding which founder's name would go on which park, the perfect solution presented itself: a coin toss using the same Portland Penny. It would be a few years after the 1845 coin toss before the city was officially founded. Portland was formally incorporated on February 8, 1851, and had by then about 800 residents, a sawmill, a log cabin hotel, and a newspaper, The Oregonian, which still exists today.

It would be another eight years before Oregon became a state, on February 14, 1859.

10. THE DAWN REDWOOD

Reference Point
The Wildwood Trail passes alongside a formal
trail head with large boulders and paving stones
that connect the trail to the turn-around at the end
of Bray Lane, a park service road.

Before we continue down to the Redwood Deck, let's pause for a look at one of the most extraordinary trees—and one of the best stories—in the whole park.

The dawn redwood is on your right as you step from the Wildwood Trail into the turn-around of the service road. There is a small black plaque mounted on a stand in front of the tree.

The story of the dawn redwood is the most unusual and amazing tale I've ever heard about a tree. It stretches around the world and more than 200 million years back in time. Dawn redwoods were once abundant throughout the world, including in Oregon. Fossils of the tree dating back millions of years have been found in Oregon's Painted Hills, and in the towns of Mitchell and Fossil, Oregon. In 2005, the same tree even became the official fossil of the State of Oregon.

The modern story starts near Tokyo, in 1941, when Miki Shigeru, a Japanese paleobotanist, discovered some five-million-year-old fossils of a new type of tree. It looked like a sequoia tree, but it was also quite different. For one thing, this new tree was a deciduous conifer, meaning that like the leaves of an oak or a maple tree, the needles on this cone-bearing tree fell off in the autumn, and the tree went dormant over the winter.

Before I started doing these hikes, I had never heard of fir trees that lose their needles; I assumed that all cone-bearing trees were evergreens. But there are actually several other examples of such trees in the park, including the bald cypress and the Japanese larch.

In the summer of 1943, Chinese forestry professor Wang Zhan was visiting the Sichuan Province when he fell ill with malaria. While he recovered, he stayed at a local agricultural school where he heard about an unusual tree that had been found in a remote eastern section of the province. It was revered by the locals, who believed that the tree had mystical powers. They had even built a temple beneath it.

Wang was intrigued, and when he was well enough, he embarked on a three-day high-mountain trek to find it. When he finally saw it, he immediately realized that it was different and special, and he collected a number of specimens. Other researchers later returned to collect additional specimens, and by 1946 they were able to match them to the fossil record that Japan's Miki Shigeru had described in 1941.

(It's surprising that the Japanese paleobotanist's discovery had become known at all in China, since the two countries were engaged in a bitter war, but science marches on.)

For scientists, the discovery of an actual, living fossil was an almost unbelievable coup, and it's been described as "a seminal botanical find of the 20th century." In the US, E.M. Merrill, the director of Harvard University's Arnold Arboretum, was eager to play a role, and in 1947 they financed another expedition to collect two kilograms of seeds. By early 1948 they were growing the trees in the Arnold Arboretum, and they distributed the remaining seeds to more 600 individuals, arboretums, and botanical gardens around the world, including here in Portland.

There's another bit of drama about the Portland trees. In the first year, to be sure that these precious seeds had the best chance to survive (and remember, very little was known about them at the time) the first seeds were sown at the arboretum's greenhouse, located on the other side of town, near Mount Tabor. There were soon about a half dozen small saplings, and they grew quickly through the summer and fall, under the watchful eye of the arboretum's curator, Ernie Fisher.

Now, this next part of the story is dramatized, but it's based on actual events:

On a wet and rainy December afternoon in 1949, Mr. Fisher was taking advantage of the nasty weather to handle some valuable "indoor work," poring over and updating an endlessly evolving catalogue in the ongoing creation of what he believed would one day be numbered among the premier arboretums in the US, when the phone rang. It was nearing the end of the day, and he was more than a little distracted by the papers on his desk.

The phone connection wasn't great, but from what he could tell, it was one of the volunteer workers over at the Mount Tabor Greenhouse.

"Mr. Fisher?" said the voice on the phone. "You know those year-old redwood saplings that you're growing over here? The Chinese trees that you like so much?"

"Yes, of course. What about them?" he replied, still mostly distracted by the paperwork.

"Well, uh," the voice started. "Well, they died. I'm just locking up here. But I threw 'em in the compost."

With that, he hung up. But now, he had Mr. Fisher's full attention.

"What?!" he said, louder now, just as the dial tone buzzed and he realized what he'd just heard.

"But...wait," he said aloud to himself...since there was no one else in the office that afternoon. "They're not dead! They're DECIDUOUS CONIFERS!"

He clicked the receiver to call back when a flash of lightning cracked almost over his head. The lights went out and the phone was dead.

He muttered to himself as he grabbed his coat and car keys....

"They've only gone dormant over the winter...it's perfectly normal for them to lose their needles now; it's almost Christmas!"

He jumped into his 1941 Plymouth and raced (as safely as he could...these are residential streets) mumbling (but not cursing...he was always a consummate professional, even when by himself) through the driving rain, down Fairview Boulevard, then through downtown and over the Hawthorne Bridge.

It was completely dark by the time he reached the greenhouse. He drove around back to shine his headlights on the compost heap, and there they were: six dawn redwoods, pulled out by the roots, lying sideways in the rain.

Carefully, gingerly, he scooped them up and took them back into the greenhouse. Luckily, none of the trunks were broken, and the roots appeared to be mostly intact. He spent the next hour carefully, lovingly replanting them into their original pots.

Next, he found some paper and some adhesive tape. He made a large sign that said:
NOT DEAD - DORMANT! DO NOT REMOVE!

He affixed his curator signature at the bottom and placed it with the trees on a separate table where he knew they would not be disturbed.

It had been no more than an hour that the young trees' bare roots had been exposed to the air. *But luckily, he thought, in December in Oregon, that air is mostly water, so they'll probably be okay.*

It would be several weeks before he had proof positive that the trees would survive, but by late April he knew that the young saplings were strong enough to plant outside and put the full spring and summer sun to work.

The first five were planted in an open area next to the rapidly growing stand of coast redwood and giant sequoia that were among the first trees planted in the park some 18 years before. These teenaged redwoods were shooting up steadily, growing several feet per year, and could already offer some protection for their younger cousins.

He saved one, however, to plant in a special spot along Fairview Boulevard, not far from the park's entrance, where he would be sure to see it every day, to keep an eye on it. (This is the tree I pointed out earlier, near the House for Summer.)

In the end, he needn't have worried. The trees took to the park like fish to water. After all, they were once native to Oregon, and the arboretum was quite possibly the best place on earth for them to thrive. They all grew straight and strong, and barely two years later, in 1952, something miraculous happened. It's explained by the plaque that was placed in front of the largest of the original dawn redwoods in April of 1999, when it was formally recognized as an Oregon Heritage Tree. It reads:

Oregon Heritage Tree Program
DAWN REDWOOD
Metasequoia glyptostroboides

When fossils of this species were first discovered in 1941 in Japan, the tree was believed to have been long extinct. Fossils were later found in the Columbia Gorge. But in 1944, live trees were found in a remote valley in central China. The Hoyt Arboretum planted seeds from these trees and in 1952, this tree became the first in the Western hemisphere to produce cones in about 6 million years."

Today this tree is taller, stronger, and better than ever, and stands as the fifth-largest dawn redwood in the Western hemisphere.

The dawn redwoods along Fischer Lane are much younger than the Heritage tree, and their sunnier, more exposed location can result in stunning fall colors

11. THE REDWOOD DECK

Reference Point
Return to the Wildwood Trail
At the end of Bray Lane
Turn left down the trail

Before the short walk to the Redwood Deck, as we return to the Wildwood Trail, take a look back toward the part of the forest that we passed through before stepping out to look at the dawn redwood. Ponder it for a moment and remember how this part of Oregon may have looked before Portland was known as Stumptown, or even before it was called The Clearing.

The reason for doing this is because we're about to do something truly extraordinary, that you can do nowhere else on earth. From here, we have the unique, exceptional opportunity to step, in just a few paces, from a typical Oregon forest into a redwood forest.

For many people, the Redwood Deck is the most beautiful, most special place in the arboretum. Yet the vast majority of people who see it have no idea how very special it really is and pass through it on the trail without fully understanding what they are seeing. That's why I like to pause for a moment, before stepping into this special stand of redwoods, and consider what we're about to do.

Reference Point
Wildwood Trail
A few steps after the end of Bray Lane
Redwood Interpretive Panel

The Redwood Interpretive Panel offers some interesting facts about these amazing trees, along with several photos of the cones, foliage, and bark of three types of redwoods found in the arboretum: the giant redwood, the coast redwood, and the dawn redwood. The panel includes a retelling of the dawn redwood story related in Chapter 10, along with a size chart with the maximum heights of redwoods.

The dawn redwood tops out at about 150 feet; the giant sequoia at 247 feet, and the coast redwood at 379 feet. The 379-foot figure refers specifically to one tree, known as Hyperion, which is the tallest tree in the world. It lives in California, about 500 miles south of here.

The immense size of these trees is difficult to grasp. The interpretive panel places drawings of the three trees next to an image of Seattle's Space Needle, at 604 feet, as a reference.

On my hikes I like to describe it differently: One of the tallest buildings in downtown Portland is the US Bank tower. We call it "big pink." On the 30th floor is the Portland Grill restaurant and bar. I often go there to enjoy the spectacular view. Once, not long ago, as I sat in one of the window seats, looking out over the city, it occurred to me that if Hyperion were growing next to this, the second tallest building in downtown Portland, its crown would extend another eight stories beyond where I sat.

After all these reference points, and especially with the awareness that we're about to do something that we can only do right here in this special place, continue down the trail's gentle slope toward the Redwood Deck. It's only about a hundred paces from the interpretive panel.

As we step into the redwood grove, notice how the whole character of the forest changes in just a few steps. If you think back to a few minutes ago, when we were in a more typical Oregon forest, there was a tangle of dense undergrowth. Here, the undergrowth is much more sparse. If you're lucky enough to be alone, notice the sounds of the environment.

Feel how the light falls on your face, breathe in the air that has a freshness to it unlike in other places. And especially, look up. Notice how very vertical everything has become. There is some kind of magic in the air here, and when you stretch your head back to look up, you realize that the magic is red and green.

Once we reach the deck, be sure to tilt your head back and look straight up. This is one of the best ways to appreciate the uniqueness of this special grove of trees. Although they are not yet the tallest trees in the arboretum (that honor belongs to a Douglas fir that is at least triple the age of these young trees) the grove of redwoods is definitely the tallest grouping of trees in any one place of the park.

It is a cathedral-like space. When early morning light filters through these beautiful trees, often with a wisp of Oregon fog, the effect is inspiring and life-affirming. And yet this amazing grove provides only a hint of the awesome beauty that you can experience in the native groves in California. The redwood forests a few hundred miles south of here are profoundly breathtaking in their beauty.

A sad statistic that I always mention is that although the California redwood groves may seem large, what remains of the original forests is only 1% of what was there before people arrived in the 1840s and began harvesting everything we could possibly remove. Fully 99% of the original redwood forest has been cut down, ravaged by rampant over-harvesting to the point that all redwoods are now severely threatened.

A fascinating fact about the deck itself is this: Some 40 years after the grove was planted, park officials realized that some of the trees had been placed too close together. For the health of the overall grove, a couple of these magnificent trees would need to be removed. But the trees were returned, in a way, because the beautiful deck we're standing on was built from the redwood of the same trees that grew right here.

View from the redwood deck

12. THE CREEK TRAIL AND BRISTLECONE PINE TRAIL

The Wildwood Trail zig-zags down the hill to a charming footbridge that spans a small creek. Johnson Creek is the name of the trickle of water that runs through the park. Not to be confused with another, much larger creek with the same name, found on Portland's East side, the arboretum's Johnson Creek usually has a flow that slows to almost nothing in the hottest days of summer. Yet in very wet months over the winter and into the spring, the volume of water can be significant. After record rains in the spring of 2017, the tiny creek overflowed its banks and even threatened to wash out Fisher Lane, the arboretum's primary road that winds through the park from SW Fairview Boulevard to West Burnside.

The flooding of that year resulted in the loss of a significant portion of the park's Creek Trail, which was closed and planted over with ground cover. The remaining section of the Creek Trail still includes one the most special sections of any trail in the park, and we will explore it shortly. But before we do, allow me to offer two bonus side trips: #1 The Oldest Tree in the arboretum, and/or #2 The Wildwood Trail to the Pittock Mansion.

I call these bonus side trips because they are not usually part of my regular tour, and I won't go into great detail about them here, but if you'd like to add 20 minutes to go and see the oldest tree, or anywhere from 45 minutes to 2 hours to do the hike up to the Pittock Mansion, check out the two bonus sections here.

Bonus 1: The Oldest Tree in the Arboretum

The arboretum's oldest tree is a bit of a detour from my regular tour, with the closest point being the small footbridge where the Creek Trail meets the Wildwood. To find the oldest tree, cross the footbridge and zig-zag up the hill on the Wildwood Trail for a short distance. Soon, you'll see a clearing farther up the hill to your left, where the Wildwood Trail meets with a connector trail that leads up to Fisher Lane, the paved road that runs through the arboretum between Fairview Boulevard and West Burnside.

Take the connector trail toward Fisher Lane. You'll pass under several more lovely dawn redwoods here, but these are much smaller than the heritage tree back by the Redwood Deck.

Cross Fisher Lane and turn right onto the White Pine Trail, which you'll take for a short distance until you see a connector trail on your left with a sign that says: "Bristlecone Pine Trail, 168 feet." Below that indication it also says: "Geographic Collection," and "Gingko Collection." Follow the connector trail to the Bristlecone Pine Trail, and turn right when you reach it. A trail sign here will say, "Picnic Area, 0.1 mile," but the oldest tree is before the picnic area, so you don't have far to go. Soon, the Bristlecone Pine Trail rejoins the White Pine Trail (which makes a loop through a lovely section of native forest), and you'll turn left here to go a few more steps. Very soon you'll see another Bristlecone Pine Trail marker reading "Bristlecone Pine Trail Parking 0.29 mi," with another indication at the bottom that says: "Oldest Doug Fir in the arboretum (Private trail) 50 ft."

A much longer side trip will take you to:

Bonus 2: Wildwood Trail to the Pittock Mansion and Beyond, to Forest Park

To find the Pittock Mansion, simply stay on the Wildwood Trail. You'll recall that I previously mentioned the blue diamond trail marking, with the mileage indicator up above. You'll find these markers every ¼ mile along the Wildwood, so it's easy to stay on track, especially between here and the Pittock Mansion, since, unlike in the rest of the arboretum (and beyond, in Forest Park) there are not a lot of other trails that intersect with the Wildwood, since the link between the arboretum and the Pittock property is a relatively narrow slice of the park.

Simply follow the signs for the Wildwood Trail as it crosses West Burnside via the beautiful Barbara Walker Crossing, and zig-zag up a steep hill for about a mile. There's a significant elevation gain of some 400 feet to reach the Pittock Mansion. If you go, it will take about a half hour to climb from the small footbridge at the lowest point or our hike in the arboretum to a spectacular viewpoint that's higher than the Overlook Trail we saw near the beginning of our visit. The view of downtown Portland is spectacular, especially on days that are clear enough for Mount Hood to dominate the landscape. Many have described it as the best view of the city you can see without a helicopter.

Note that since the hike is uphill for virtually the entire way, it can be a bit tiring to go, especially since the return hike will take you back down to one of the lowest points in the arboretum before the return to the arboretum's Visitor Center. The Pittock Mansion is easily accessible by car, but be aware that there are no buses nearby. From the mansion you can walk back, or if you have a lot of time, keep going along with Wildwood and hike all day long into Forest Park. As previously mentioned, the Wildwood Trail is the longest urban hiking trail in North America, and after the Pittock Mansion, it runs some 20 miles farther into the 5,000 acres of Forest Park. But that's a topic for another book.

For either bonus trip, you can easily retrace your steps along the Wildwood Trail to the charming wooden footbridge that crosses the creek, and resume the hike to enjoy the last few highlights of the arboretum.

From the bridge, then, the Creek Trail continues up a gentle slope, with the creek to our right, while the Wildwood trail extends in the other direction. Here, we'll continue along the Creek Trail, where we get another spectacular view of the redwood grove. Just a few steps beyond the footbridge, look to your left to discover that we're now at the bottom of the arboretum's redwood grove. Here, again, we have a completely different perspective on these magnificent trees.

In total, there are 77 giant redwoods and 43 coast redwoods in this part of the park, according to the online database that the arboretum maintains. The vast majority of them were planted in 1931.

Since I live just a short distance away, I've had the pleasure, over more than two decades, to experience these trees in all kinds of weather. From the coldest winter days when the roads and trails are covered with a half-inch sheet of ice and it's hazardous to walk anywhere, to the hottest days of summer, when the creek has dried to nothing more than a damp line in the creekbed. (Such summer days particularly amaze me, because despite the almost complete absence of water, the temperature still drops by some 10 degrees in this part of the park, as if the mere memory of flowing water nearby were enough to cool the forest.)

At any and every time of year, this small section of the arboretum's redwood grove is an inspiring and refreshing place to visit. Stay for a few minutes and notice how the light filters through the tall trees, and how a gentle breeze meanders among the branches. It's truly a magical place.

As we continue up the Creek Trail, notice again how the forest quickly returns to a more typical Oregon setting. Once again, in just a few steps, we are transported from one type of forest to another, and here, along the creek, is an excellent place to see a number of native plants, including the sword fern and maidenhair fern with its distinctive black stems. Also found along the creek are numerous salal plants, a bushy native plant that produces edible berries of a dark-blue to black color. These were harvested by the local Chinook people who preserved them as a valuable food source over the cold winter months.

In a few steps we will cross another small footbridge, and not far beyond, the trail will widen to allow us to see the amazing root system of an old Western hemlock that holds back a large section of the hillside. It's called "the root tree," for reasons that are obvious once you see it. Although the roots of this tree are not so different from those of any other Western hemlock, thanks to the steep hillside, we get to see its extensive root system on an almost vertical plane.

Unfortunately, this tree suffered after it was struck by another tree and was unable to survive the record heat of the summer of 2017. Although the tree itself is dead, expert arborists have carefully sculpted it so that it will decay safely and gradually, and the root system will remain in place for many years, since it is an especially impressive sight.

From the root tree, we will take the short, steep trail up to Fisher Lane and walk straight across to the branch of the Bristlecone Pine Trail that turns left and goes up the hill immediately after you step off the road. At first, it appears to run parallel to Fisher Lane. Actually, it zig-zags up the hill. Pause for a moment at the first hairpin turn, which zigs tightly around to the right. At the apex of the curve, turn and look straight across Fisher Lane. Here you'll see that we're standing directly across from a double Douglas fir, like the lover tree that we saw on the first half of our visit—except this pair of trees hasn't been manhandled in any way; they've grown naturally, probably for more than a hundred years.

This is how the lover tree *should* look. It's the natural, healthy appearance of countless similar examples of Douglas fir double trees in forests across the Pacific Northwest.

If you look closely at the base, it looks like a single enormous tree trunk. But from there, we can see that at about 10 feet up, the massive trunk clearly separates into two distinct trees. The tree on the right is substantially larger than the tree on the left; it's probably twenty or more years older, and since it's on the south side, it has always gotten better exposure to sunlight than its partner tree to the north.

We can learn a lot from this double tree, and we can get an even better view of it if we proceed another approximately 40 to 45 paces up the trail, where we can look at the tree from the same angle, but from a slightly higher and longer vantage point.

From here we can easily see the whole tree. Notice the perfect symmetry; the two trunks actually function together as a single tree. And in fact, if I hadn't pointed it out to you, there's a very good chance that you would never have noticed it. Before starting these hikes a few years ago, I had lived nearby and walked or driven directly past this magnificent double tree literally hundreds of times without ever seeing it. It's only after I started these hikes that it popped out for me.

Scientists have made significant progress in understanding how trees communicate and work cooperatively together in forests, actively sharing resources with one another in ways that are nothing short of astonishing. One example of this is to consider the two trunks before us. Look to the very top of the tree. You'll see that the leading, highest branch at the crown of the larger trunk is virtually the same height, within inches of that of the smaller trunk.

Yet it's clear that as individual trees, the southern trunk is significantly older, perhaps by some 20 years or more. During their early years together, the two trees would have competed for light and resources. And with its placement on the south side, the larger tree could easily have overpowered the younger sapling, starving it of light. Since we know that Douglas fir leaves are relatively inefficient at photosynthesis, it's surprising that the smaller tree survived at all.

Unless…

My personal hypothesis about this pair of remarkably healthy and clearly cooperating Douglas fir trees is based on the work of Canadian forest ecologist Suzanne Simard. Her 2016 TED Talk entitled "How Trees Talk to Each Other" described the groundbreaking discoveries she made in over 30 years of research in the forests of British Columbia. Much of her research involved Douglas fir trees in forests located within 350 miles of Portland, in an ecosystem that is essentially identical to the forests of Oregon.

The conclusions from her research are nothing short of life altering. I actually wept during part of her talk, which I will not attempt to explain. Instead, I strongly encourage you to watch her presentation at: https://tinyurl.com/ v6wxmor or Google "Suzanne Simard TED Talk" and it will appear.

Her research proves definitively that trees not only communicate and share resources with one another, but that they can actually recognize each other. Certain large, established trees (which she affectionately calls "mother trees") actually nurture smaller trees via a vast, incredibly dense network of fungus known as mycelium. Her experiments even proved that mother trees send resources on a preferential basis to their own offspring.

I believe that DNA analysis will one day confirm that the smaller trunk of this perfect double tree is in fact the offspring of the larger tree, which has nurtured and supported the smaller tree from the beginning. This explains why it has survived and thrived despite otherwise fatal placement quite literally beneath an overwhelmingly larger competing tree.

Before we leave this unusual viewpoint, there is a fascinating view of another special Douglas fir that is also visible from this same spot. To find it, look again at the double tree. Just to the left of it, literally a thumb's width to the left, is another Doug fir; however, since it is farther away, and on the other side of the creek, it appears to be about 3/4 the height of the double tree.

Now, here's a secret: If you look carefully, you'll see the crown of a third tall Douglas fir, much farther (about 400 feet) in the distance. If you're standing in just the right place, it can be seen directly between the double tree and the tall tree to its left. This third tree is actually about the same height as both of the others, but its crown is not nearly as full or filled out as the other trees in our immediate, much closer view.

That's because this is the lightning tree, which we will visit in just a few minutes. However, it's really interesting to see it from this perspective, since it allows us to compare its crown to the other trees of a similar age. The reason its crown looks so sparse and sickly (in fact, it bears an almost uncanny resemblance to Charlie Brown's Christmas tree, unable to hold even one ornament) is because it is entirely new growth after the top 20 feet of this tree was sheared off by a massive bolt of lightning during a 1982 electrical storm that almost split the giant tree in half!

The lightning tree is the last stop on our tour, but from the base, it's impossible to see the crown. From here, however, you can easily compare the damaged crown to the healthy crowns of massive, similar trees of the same age in a direct line of sight—something that you can't do from anywhere else in the park.

Continue up this short trail to the paved section of the Bristlecone Pine Trail. If you simply walk straight up the trail, you'll walk right into the next interesting tree, and one the most unusual trees in the park, a monkey puzzle tree. This is an ancient tree that comes from Chile, where it is endangered. Go ahead and carefully touch the leaves. They are stiff and prickly, but if you are careful and handle them gently, you won't hurt yourself.

The rather absurd name comes from an Englishman who, upon encountering the tree for the first time, and feeling the prickly leaves, is reported to have said, "I'll bet a monkey would have a real puzzle trying to climb that tree!" Or words to that effect. Personally, I find the story ridiculous, but it does illustrate a valid point about how most trees received their common name, which is to say, in a word, randomly.

The monkey puzzle tree's strange leaves were eaten by dinosaurs

Throughout this hike I have used the common names for the trees and other plants we have visited based on the assumption that is true for myself and that I believe to be true for most people, that the Latinized, scientific names are too long, clunky, difficult to say, read, spell, or remember, and for all these reasons, are not useful in normal conversation. The great thing about the arboretum, however, is that on all of the trees that have an identifying plaque, you'll also find the specific scientific name, so you can easily learn more about it.

Turning from the monkey puzzle tree, walk along the paved path toward the small parking lot. Up ahead we'll see the trees for which the trail is named, the bristlecone pine trees. I used to think of these small, scrubby, and even somewhat unhealthy-looking trees as not very attractive. Until one day, from a short distance away, standing next to the monkey puzzle tree, I pointed them out to a visitor. She almost gasped when she saw them and said how beautiful they looked.

Immediately I saw them in a different light. From a short distance away, the rugged appearance of these ancient trees is downright poetic. And although when you get close, they still have an almost sickly appearance when compared to the lush greenery of so many trees in the rest of the park, be assured that these trees are quite healthy. Their native habitat is in the rocky high deserts of California, Nevada, and Utah, where they are among the oldest living things on Earth. The oldest known living tree is a bristlecone pine in California that has been named Methuselah, after the biblical character in the book of Genesis. According to the Bible, he lived to be 969 years old. The age of the Methuselah tree is much greater, at more than 4,850 years.

Curiously, as I was confirming the facts for this chapter (thanks to Wikipedia, which is an amazing resource and my go-to source for many of the facts and figures I've shared) I came across another oldest tree article about a Norway spruce tree in Sweden. It was found to be more than 9,500 years old. (The arboretum's collection of Norway spruce trees is one of its most impressive, and we're about to step into a Norway spruce forest.) However, that oldest tree is a clonal tree, growing from ancient roots, as opposed to a unique, individual tree. An ancient stand of quaking aspen clonal trees in Utah is believed to be as much as a million years old.

The Methuselah bristlecone pine in the White Mountains of California is believed to be the oldest living individual tree in the world.

Reference Point
From the parking lot at the trailhead
of the Bristlecone Pine Trail, turn right
onto Fisher Lane, and walk up the hill
and around the curve, stopping at
the Bamboo Garden.

13. JAPANESE LARCH, THE BAMBOO FOREST, AND THE NORWEGIAN WOOD

Standing at the entrance to the Bamboo Forest look up and behind us to the right. Here, we are standing beneath a number of Japanese larch trees. Like the dawn redwood trees we saw earlier, these are also deciduous conifers. In the fall their needles turn a distinct yellow before they fall and create a deep and very rich mulch that surrounds and piles up around them, providing nutrients over the winter when sunlight is in short supply.

The Bamboo Forest is a relatively recent addition to the park, as of 2016, but since bamboo is literally the fastest-growing plant in the world, it already has the feel of a well-established corner of the arboretum. With some 30 different species and more than 100 individual plants, it's been called the largest collection of bamboo in the Pacific Northwest. Bamboo isn't a tree, however; it's actually a grass. Under the right conditions, a bamboo plant can grow up to three feet in a day!

In the center of the Bamboo Forest is the arboretum's only other art installation. We saw the House for Summer near the viewpoint. This large metal sphere is called a "Basket of Air," by the Portland Artist Ivan McLean. If you look him up online, you'll find that he's created several similar sculptures, but this one is unique because of the support structure he created for it, fashioned to look like bamboo stalks.

Bamboo is known to be quite invasive, but although it grows up fast, it spreads out slowly, and you'll notice that the arboretum's bamboo forest is well contained, completely surrounded by paved roads.

Continuing up the hill on Fisher Lane from the Bamboo Forest, we'll immediately come to another service road. This is Bray Lane, named after Jim Bray, who was curator after Ernie Fisher. (Fisher was curator from 1940 to 1970; Bray took over after Fisher retired.)

At the entrance to Bray Lane, you'll see that vehicular traffic is blocked by a series of removable posts. Immediately to the left of these posts is a large boulder. Stand directly in front of the boulder and look straight down the lane. Now look up at the treetops.

From this vantage point, you'll have another straight-line view of the crown of the lightning tree, which pokes out from the middle of the grove of Norway spruce. The fact that the mature Douglas fir was so much taller than the surrounding Norway spruce trees is probably why it was struck by lightning in the first place. As a lone tree towering above the surrounding canopy, it's practically the definition of a lightning rod.

This view is quite a bit closer, about twice as close as the view we had from the double tree, and we can see more clearly how different the top of this tree is when compared to other, uninjured trees.

There are several reasons why the canopy of this tree is so spare when compared to the many healthy treetops nearby. The main reason, however, is because of the huge wound the lightning inflicted on the entire tree. Most of the healing energy in the early years went toward repairing the giant gash that runs the length of the whole tree. This great old Douglas Fir is healthy today, and if it can avoid getting struck again, it can survive and thrive for several hundred more years.

From entrance to Bray Lane, it's a short walk up the hill on Fisher Lane to a connector trail on the left that goes to the Spruce Trail and into the arboretum's impressive stand of Norway spruce. Alternatively, it's just a few more steps farther up the hill along Fisher Lane to the trailhead of the Spruce Trail. Here we'll pause at the final interpretive panel of our hike, entitled simply "Spruce."

As with the other informational panels throughout the park, the Spruce Panel is packed with interesting details about these beautiful trees, including photos and drawings that highlight five different varieties among the many spruce trees currently found in the arboretum.

When it was established in March of 1928, the original plan for the park was to be a conifer arboretum. It was during these early years that collections of pine, fir, and cedar were planted, including the substantial forest of redwoods, and an even larger selection of spruce trees. In all, there are more than 330 individual trees and at least 34 different species of spruce trees in the park, which is more than half of all spruce species in the world.

In total, the arboretum's world class collection of conifers includes 237 different species with many large, mature specimens that are unmatched by other gardens around the country. The largest collection of any one species of spruce is the more than 90 mature Norway spruce planted along the first section of the Spruce Trail, with most of them dating to 1931.

These are the same trees found in the Black Forest of Germany, and once again, for the second time in the last hour, we have the unique opportunity to do something that you can only do here in the arboretum. For this is the only place on earth where you can step from an Oregon forest into a miniature Black Forest of Germany.

As with the redwood grove, notice how the understory will suddenly become completely different. The dense Norway spruce block out a lot of light, allowing for little vegetation to grow. Walking through this section of the park in winter on a cold, foggy afternoon, the light can seem fragile and the woods feel very dark and foreboding. It makes it easy to understand how the Black Forest of Germany got its name, and how it inspired generations of people living in and around it to invent frightening folktales to keep children from running off and getting lost in the woods.

If you think about the Grimm fairy tales such as Hansel and Gretel, Little Red Riding Hood, Snow White, or Sleeping Beauty, in all of these stories the dark, dangerous forest plays a significant role. You could even say that the forest itself is a primary character. Walking through Portland's miniature Black Forest can give you a better appreciation fo the fairy tales you heard growing up.

From 2011 to 2017 there was a popular television program that was made in Portland called Grimm. It was (very) loosely based on the Grimm fairy tales, with all kinds of frightening monsters and old-world beasts and goblins doing battle with the Portland police department. A portion of at least one episode was filmed in the arboretum; they even installed an entire cemetery on the hillside next to the Stevens Pavilion just up the hill from this stand of Norway spruce.

An interesting fact about the Norway spruce tree relates to its bark. As trees grow, the outer layer has to expand to accommodate the increasing size of the trunk, and every species of tree has its own the solution to the problem. Earlier, we saw how the bark of a Himalayan birch falls off in sheets that look like paper. The much denser bark of a Norway spruce is more rigid, and as the trunk expands, it sheds chunks that resemble jigsaw puzzle pieces, falling off and creating natural wood chips around the trees.

14. THE LIGHTNING TREE

As we walk along the Spruce Trail beneath the dark canopy of Norway spruce, the main trail makes a long, gentle curve around to the left, while another, unmarked path heads straight up a short rise to a small plateau with a couple of dozen additional spruce trees and Fisher Lane just beyond.

Before we climb that little rise to make our way back to the Visitor Center and the main entrance to the park, however, stay on the main trail as it completes the curve. Just beyond, you'll see the large trunk of a big old Douglas fir. The trunk is significantly larger than any of the surrounding spruce trees. The small black plaque on the tree identifies it with a capital N, a native tree that was probably already 100 years old when the Norway spruce were planted here in 1931. Be aware that it's easy to walk right past it if you're not paying attention, since it carries no markings to say that it is the lightning tree.

But if you look closely, you'll also notice a wide area of trail, about the size and shape of a pitcher's mound, that circles around to the back side of the tree. This is where you must look in order to see what is truly unusual about this particular Douglas fir. From here, you'll have the unique opportunity to see the damage that remains from the huge injury the tree sustained when it was struck by lightning in 1982.

If you follow this wide gash up the tree, you'll see that the huge jolt of electrical energy did not travel in a straight line as went to ground. If it had, it could easily have split the tree in half and knocked some or all of it down to the ground.

Instead, as you follow the gash up the tree as high as you can, you'll see that the energy came down in long spiral. The very top of the tree was essentially vaporized; perhaps as much as 20 feet of the tree's canopy was destroyed in an instant.

The massive electric surge spiraled down, creating a tremendous wound on the tree that stretches from the back side at our vantage point on the ground, up and around to the opposite side of the tree some 150 feet in the air.

As soon as it was struck, the tree began to heal itself, creating a natural bandage of sap and other substances to cover the wound, and begin the decades-long process of repair.

In 1982 the width of the gash was as much as two feet across; by the year 2020 the damaged gash was only half as wide. It appears to be closing itself with increasing speed.

Given enough time, this tree will one day be completely healed, and could even become almost indistinguishable from other Doug firs of similar age. There are reports of loggers who harvested large old trees like this one, only to find when cutting them open that there was a big swath of bark on the inside of the tree.

Such internal bark was the result of a lightning strike some 50 to 200 or more years earlier. Lightning is surprisingly common, more so than you might imagine. It strikes somewhere on earth more than 40 times per second, but mostly (70%) in the tropics, where there's much more interplay between warm and cool air.

This tree most likely attracted the lightning strike because it dared poke its head out above the shorter, younger spruce trees. Norway spruce can grow up to 180 feet tall; Douglas firs can reach up to 330 feet along the coast; many in the arboretum are well above 200 feet.

The lightning tree marks the last stop of the hike, but there are still many more things to see. This book has covered only about one quarter of the total 12 miles of trails that run through the arboretum, and I have plans for more books to cover the rest of the park.

From the lightning tree it's easy to find your way back to the Visitor Center. Follow the Spruce Trail back to Fisher Lane, or climb the unmarked path mentioned earlier up to the small plateau. From there, another steep rise of only four or five steps uphill will take you to the top of Fisher Lane. Cross the lane and follow the Fir Trail as it runs parallel to SW Fairview Boulevard, toward the Stevens Pavilion, the large open shelter with picnic tables, which is directly across Fairview Boulevard from the Visitor Center.

Be sure to check out the Visitor Center and its gift shop, filled with many interesting books and souvenirs, as well as a calendar of events and activities that go on all year. You can also visit the arboretum's website at www.hoytarboretum.org to learn more about its history and check out the online plant database for detailed information on all the trees and many other plants, along with an interactive map that shows their locations in the park.

Thank you for taking this hike with me. I hope you've enjoyed it as much as I have!

David Boe
January, 2020

15. ACKNOWLEDGEMENTS

The primary reason this book exists is because Portland has an arboretum to begin with. Its creation was due to the efforts of many foresighted Portlanders of the 1920s; none more so than Multnomah County Commissioner Ralph Warren Hoyt, whose work in 1928 was so determinative that the park was named in his honor.

The Arboretum is a multi-generational gift from the past to Portland's future, and the fact that it exists at all is the result of one small miracle after another. Consider its location. The 189 acre site sits less than 3 miles from the center of downtown, surrounded by some of the most expensive residential real estate in the Pacific Northwest.

There have been pressures from literally all sides of the park to whittle away at it over the years, and as recently as the 1980s the park was considered by some to be open land. The dedication of an 11 acre portion of the park as Portland's Vietnam Memorial led to the creation of Hoyt Arboretum Friends, a membership based 501(c)(3) nonprofit that now works closely with Portland Parks and Recreation to assure the continuing operation of the park. For this book, in addition to my beloved canine pal Buddy, who has been a constant support and inspiration in creating this book, I must add the highest praise to Joan Rogers, whose editorial genius and inspiring encouragement were instrumental in getting this project over the finish line. The final polish and the resulting glow is hers. Thank you, Joan.

16. DISCLAIMER

This book is intended to offer helpful information on the topics discussed. The publisher and author are not responsible for any specific recommendations and are not liable for any damages or negative consequences from any suggestions or advice, to any person reading or following the information in this book. References are provided for informational purposes only and do not constitute endorsement of any websites or other sources. Readers should be aware that the websites listed in this book may change without notice.

www.ingramcontent.com/pod-product-compliance
Lightning Source LLC
Chambersburg PA
CBHW061251040426
42444CB00010B/2346